Lydia

Written by **Marty Rhodes Figley**

Illustrated by **Anita Riggio**

EERDMANS BOOKS FOR YOUNG READERS
GRAND RAPIDS, MICHIGAN   CAMBRIDGE, U.K.

C
E
Fig

For my daughter Meg, who knows how to be a good friend — M. R. F.
To Bailey, Lydia, Andy, July, and in memory of Eloise — A. R.

Text copyright ©1999 by Marty Rhodes Figley
Illustrations copyright © 1999 by Anita Riggio

Published 1999 by Eerdmans Books for Young Readers
an imprint of Wm. B. Eerdmans Publishing Co.
255 Jefferson Ave. S.E.
Grand Rapids, Michigan 49503
P.O. Box 163, Cambridge CB3 9PU U.K.

Printed in Hong Kong

03 02 01 00 99   7 6 5 4 3 2 1

LIBRARY OF CONGRESS CATALOGING-IN-PUBLICATION DATA
Figley, Marty Rhodes, 1948-
Lydia / by Marty Figley; illustrated by Anita Riggio.
p. cm.
ISBN 0-8028-5141-X (pbk.: alk. paper)
1. Bible stories, English — N.T. Acts.   2. Lydia (Biblical character) — Juvenile literature.
I. Riggio, Anita, ill.   II. Title.
BS2595.5.F54 1998
226.6 — DC20   *96-21210*
                                             CIP
                                             AC

The illustrations were done in watercolor.
The text was set in Usherwood Book.
The book was designed by Joy Chu.

L ydia loved purple.

She loved
purple flowers,

purple shadows
at dusk,

and purple fruit like
plums and grapes.

She wore purple skirts, purple blouses,
and sometimes tied a purple ribbon
in her hair.

To make a living, she sold purple dyes and cloth to people. Whenever someone bought something purple, Lydia was happy.

"You will love this purple fabric," she would say. And Lydia meant it, because anything purple was precious to her.

Sometimes she would walk through her house
and admire all her beautiful purple things:
her purple walls, her purple chairs, and
her purple rug.

"Perfectly purple," Lydia would say.
"Everything clean and tidy and purple."

Lydia loved purple — but she also loved God.
She and her friends would meet to worship
together.

One morning Lydia put on her best purple
outfit and met her friends down by the river.

After she spread a purple blanket on the grass, she knelt and prayed, "Please, God, show me the way."

As she prayed, two strangers appeared. They were Paul and Silas, the Christian missionaries.

Paul began telling Lydia and her friends about God and His son, Jesus. "I didn't know about Jesus and his love," said Lydia, "but because of you, Paul and Silas, I now do."

She found some purple flowers on the riverbank and handed them to Paul. "Thank you for showing me the way," she said.

Lydia was baptized, and she and her friends became Christians.

Now they needed a place indoors
to meet. Lydia had a great idea—
Paul and Silas could use her house for
meetings! There everything was clean and
tidy and perfectly purple.

When Lydia told Paul and Silas her idea,
Paul was pleased.

"Lydia, you are a kind and generous
woman," he said.

At first Lydia looked forward to these meetings and would rush home from work to get ready for them. She would shake out her purple rug.

Next she would arrange her purple furniture.

Then she would set out the refreshments —
grapes, bread, and cheese on her best purple plates.

News of the meetings began to spread, and Lydia's house was often crowded with people. They listened to Paul preach about Jesus and tell stories of His amazing love.

This made Lydia very happy.

But after a while, Lydia looked around
at her beloved purple things and sighed.
They would never be the same because of
the meetings.

People leaned against her purple walls and left
hand prints on them. When they ate, they spilled
bread crumbs on her purple chairs and dropped
grapes that got squished into her purple rug.

And now three of her best purple plates were broken. This made Lydia sad, because her purple things were precious to her.

"Nothing is clean and tidy anymore," she said.

So she decided to talk to Paul about meeting somewhere else.

But she couldn't find Paul, even though she looked all over town.

Finally she asked one of her friends where Paul was. Lydia's friend grabbed her arm.

"Haven't you heard? Paul and Silas were thrown into prison for preaching about Jesus."

Lydia rushed back to her house.

But she didn't notice any of her
precious things —
    not her purple walls,
    not her purple chairs,
    not her purple rug.
She was worried about Paul and Silas
stuck in that awful prison.

Several days passed. Then one night, when Lydia and her friends were gathered at her house, the purple walls began to shake.

They were afraid. What was going on?

They all began to pray. Lydia especially prayed
for the safety of Paul and Silas.

The next day there was a knock at
Lydia's door.

When she opened it, she
discovered Paul and Silas. They were
dusty and tired — but smiling.

"God caused an earthquake," Paul
said. "It opened the prison doors, and
now we are free."

Lydia was happy. Her prayers had been
answered!

She grabbed one of her best pieces of purple cloth and wiped the dust from their faces.

Lydia smiled and said, "Friends, not purple things, are most precious of all."